BERNSTEIN
BROADWAY PIANO SOLOS

WEST SIDE STORY

ISBN 978-1-4803-9676-0

The name and likeness of "Leonard Bernstein" is a registered trademark of Amberson Holdings LLC.
Used by Permission

LEONARD
BERNSTEIN
Music Publishing
Company LLC

BOOSEY & HAWKES

AN IMAGEM COMPANY

DISTRIBUTED BY

HAL•LEONARD®
CORPORATION
7777 W. BLUEMOUND RD. P.O. BOX 13819 MILWAUKEE, WI 53213

www.leonardbernstein.com
www.boosey.com
www.halleonard.com

BERNSTEIN
BROADWAY PIANO SOLOS

AMERICA
from WEST SIDE STORY

Lyrics by STEPHEN SONDHEIM
Music by LEONARD BERNSTEIN
Arranged by Carol Klose

Brightly, with a strong beat

COOL
from WEST SIDE STORY

Lyrics by STEPHEN SONDHEIM
Music by LEONARD BERNSTEIN
Arranged by Carol Klose

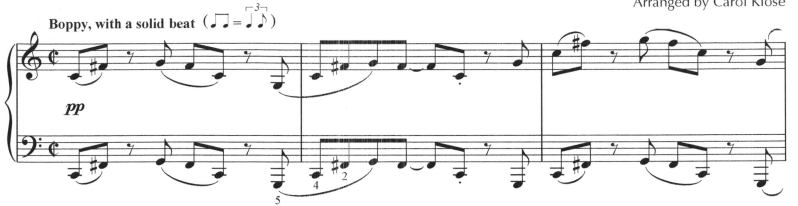

I FEEL PRETTY

from WEST SIDE STORY

Lyrics by STEPHEN SONDHEIM
Music by LEONARD BERNSTEIN
Arranged by Carol Klose

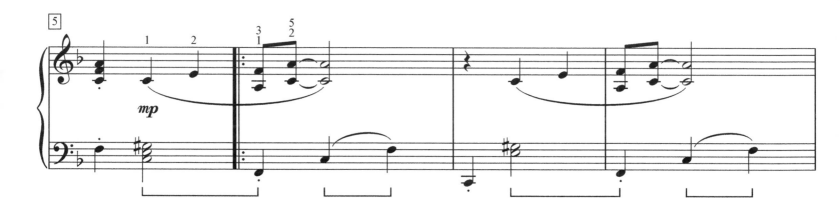

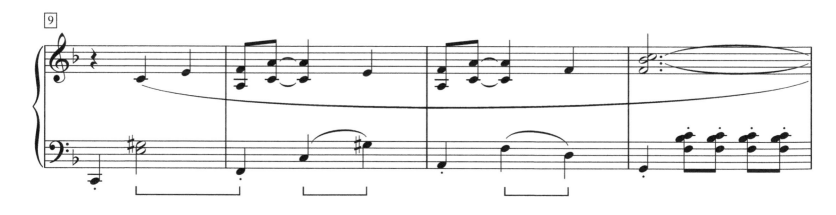

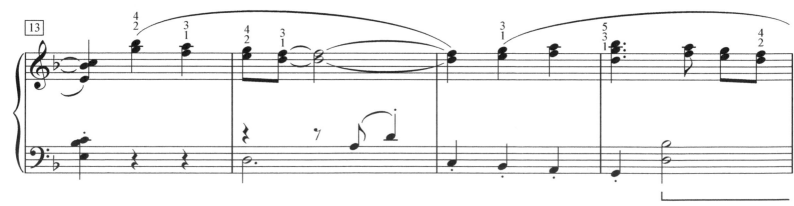

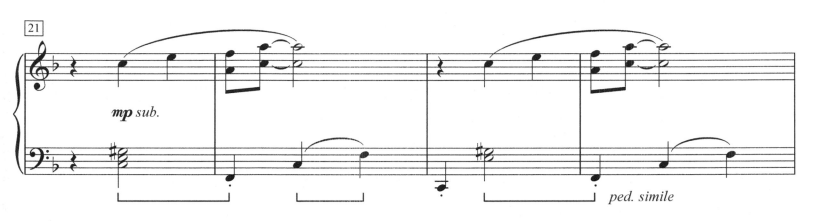

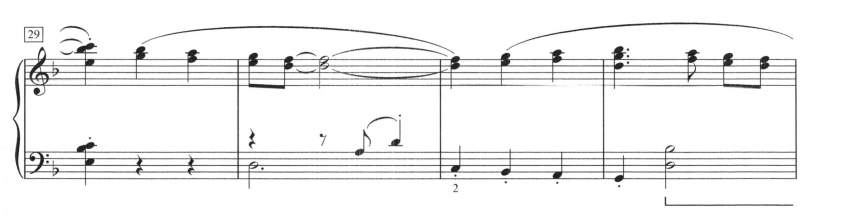

MAKE OUR GARDEN GROW

from CANDIDE

Lyrics by RICHARD WILBUR
Music by LEONARD BERNSTEIN
Arranged by Rachel Chapin

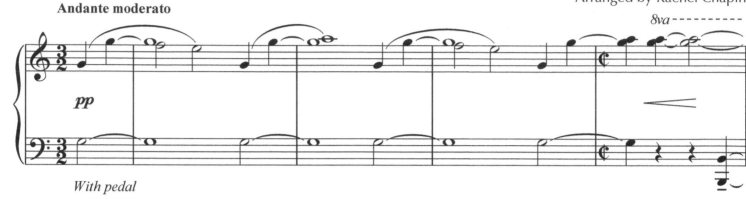

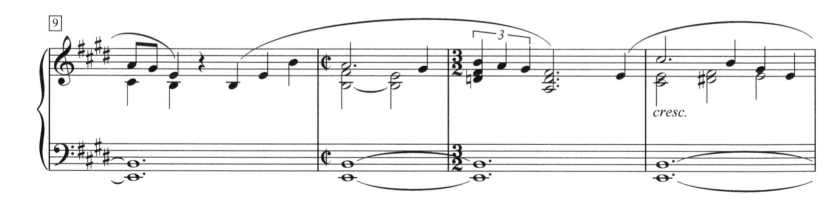

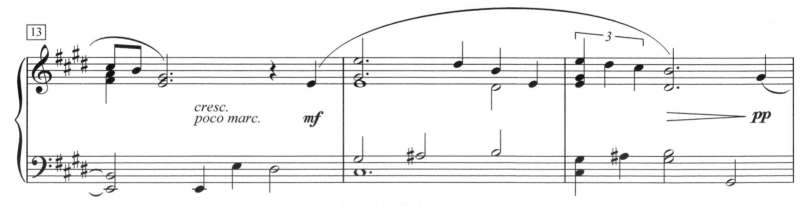

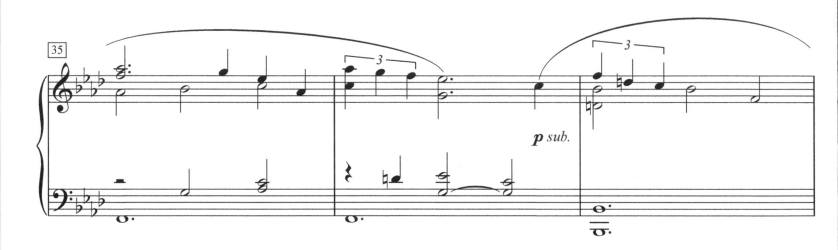

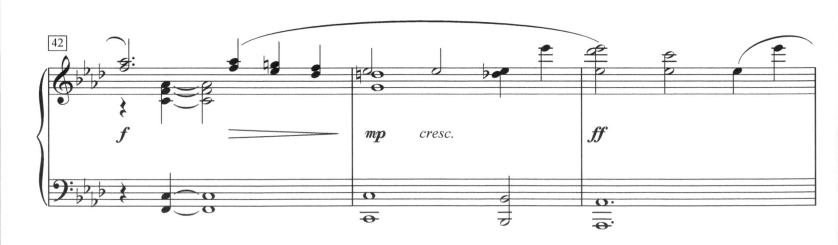

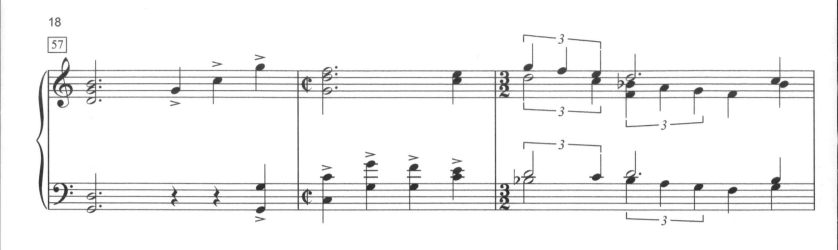

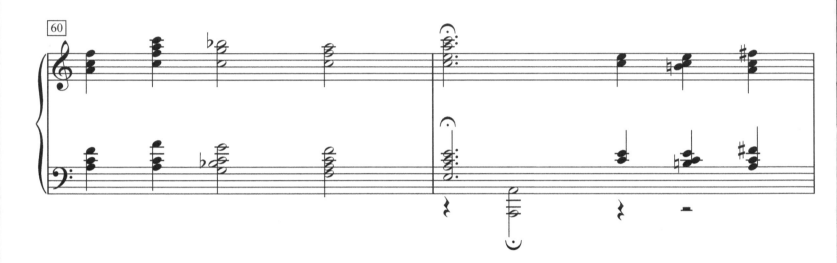

Maestoso molto

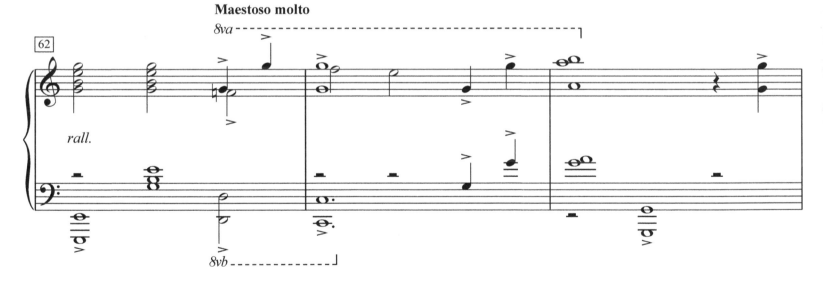

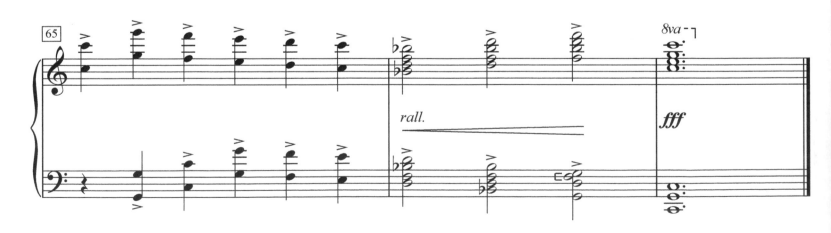

LONELY TOWN
from ON THE TOWN

Lyrics by BETTY COMDEN and ADOLPH GREEN
Music by LEONARD BERNSTEIN
Arranged by Rachel Chapin

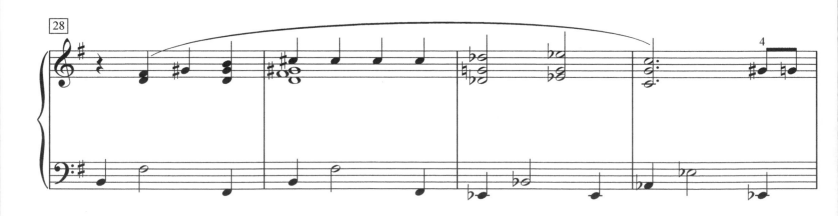

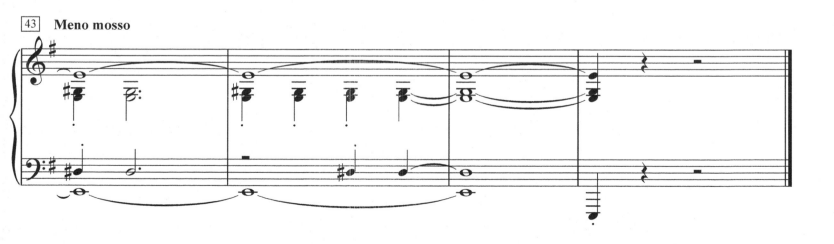

MARIA
from WEST SIDE STORY

Lyrics by STEPHEN SONDHEIM
Music by LEONARD BERNSTEIN
Arranged by Carol Klose

NEW YORK, NEW YORK

from ON THE TOWN

Lyrics by BETTY COMDEN and ADOLPH GREEN
Music by LEONARD BERNSTEIN
Arranged by Rachel Chapin

SOME OTHER TIME

from ON THE TOWN

Lyrics by BETTY COMDEN and ADOLPH GREEN
Music by LEONARD BERNSTEIN
Arranged by Rachel Chapin

Freely, with sentiment

TAKE CARE OF THIS HOUSE
from 1600 PENNSYLVANIA AVENUE

Lyrics by ALAN JAY LERNER
Music by LEONARD BERNSTEIN
Arranged by Rachel Chapin

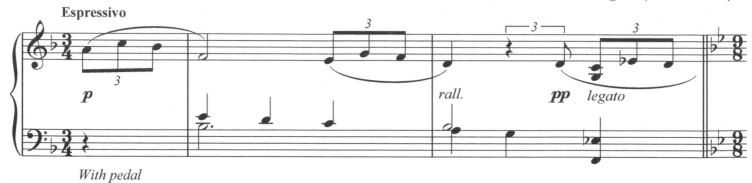

TONIGHT
from WEST SIDE STORY

Lyrics by STEPHEN SONDHEIM
Music by LEONARD BERNSTEIN
Arranged by Carol Klose

Steady Latin beat

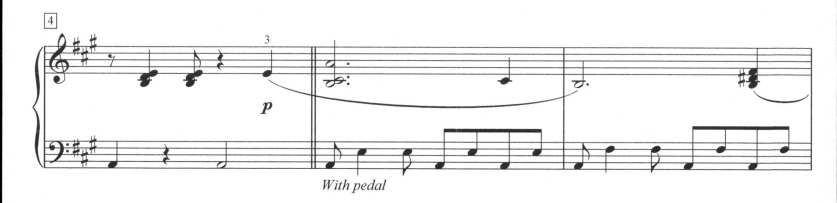

With pedal

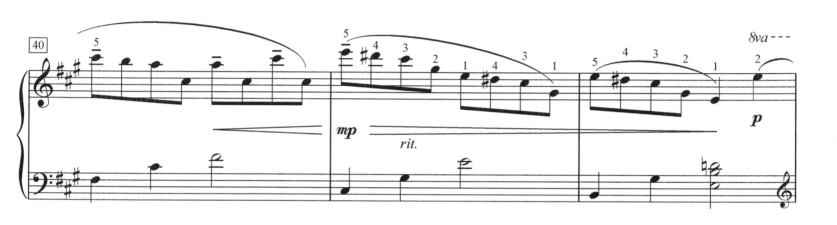

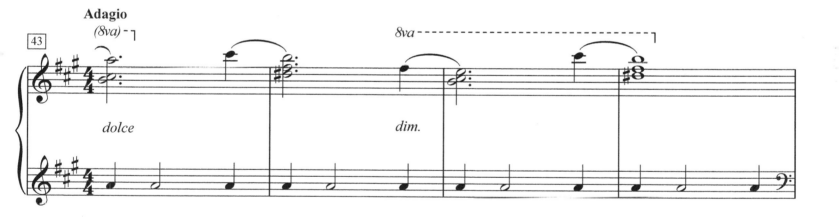

THE WRONG NOTE RAG
from WONDERFUL TOWN

Music by LEONARD BERNSTEIN
Lyrics by BETTY COMDEN and ADOLPH GREEN
Arranged by Rachel Chapin

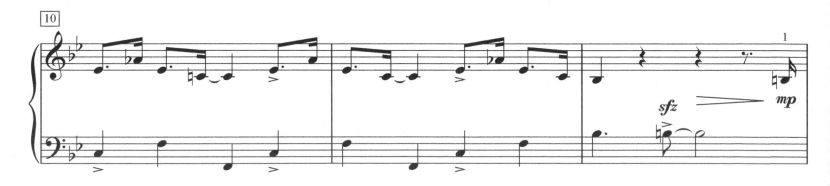

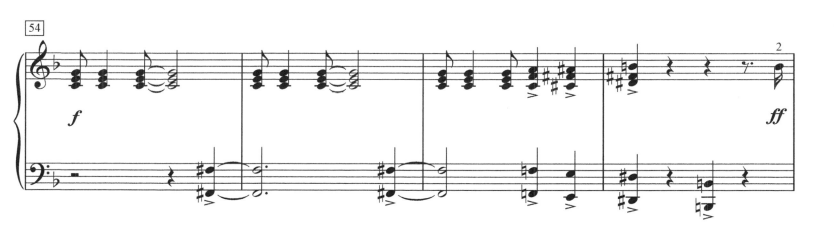

SOMEWHERE
from WEST SIDE STORY

Lyrics by STEPHEN SONDHEIM
Music by LEONARD BERNSTEIN
Arranged by Carol Klose

Poco più mosso

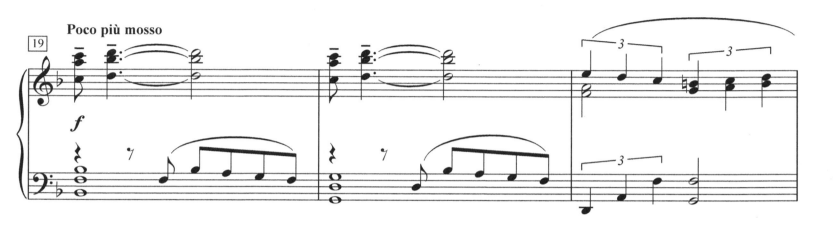

Tempo I